*E*ver wonder what
your employees think
about your leadership
style? Would they say it's
too demanding, too
bureaucratic? Would they
be willing to do more for
you?
Get ready for some
straight answers.

PAY ATTENTION, IMPROVE, AND GUIDE

DAVID COTTRELL

The  Company

To order additional copies of
Listen Up, Leader!
or for information on other
WALK THE TALK® products and services,
contact us at
1.888.822.9255
or visit our website at
www.walkthetalk.com

*Helping organizations achieve success
through Ethical Leadership and
Values-Based Business Practices*

Listen Up, Leader! Second Edition

        The WALK THE TALK Company
        2925 LBJ Freeway, Suite 201
        Dallas, Texas 75234
        972.243.8863

Printed in the United States of America
10 9 8 7

ISBN 1-885228-37-6

Listen (lis'en) v.
1. To apply oneself to hearing something.
2. To pay attention; give heed.

Up (up) adv.
1. From a lower to a higher position.
2. In or toward a more advanced state.
3. So as to increase or improve.

Leader (lē'der) n.
1. A person who leads others along a way;
   a guide.

Listen up!
We've got something to say!

First of all, we're overachievers!

Surprised? In your eyes we may look like average employ-ees, but away from work we excel at many things!

And although you're our manager, supervisor, or team leader, for the most part you haven't discovered what it takes to motivate us to over-achieve at work.

Sure, you probably think we're good. Chances are we wouldn't still be here if we weren't. And hopefully you see that we're dependable, trustworthy, and that we usually do the job without much complaining or causing trouble. That's all true. But the fact is that we could do so much more for both you and this organization.

With the right leadership from you, we could overachieve in our jobs the same way we do in other aspects of our lives.

When it comes to our children, for example, we have a passion to help them become successful in life, and we'll do whatever it takes to give them that opportunity. Our wives/husbands believe we would sacrifice everything for them, and they're right! We're involved in our places of worship. We're active in everything from Little Leagues to bowling leagues. And we often jump at the chance to take the lead in activities that are important to us and our families.

Why, then, are we "just average, everyday employees" when we could be so much more? Maybe you haven't helped us to be more. You know, we all could be the committed, energetic, dynamic employees you've dreamed about if you'd just take the time to LISTEN.

> We could be so much more than just numbers to you. Yet you've never really asked us to be anything else!

Don't be offended. This book could have been written for any of the millions of people who have chosen leadership careers. We're writing this so that you can understand how, by working together, we can all increase our job satisfaction and ultimately achieve more success.

A lot of changes have occurred in the recent past. So many of our fellow workers have left to work for other companies, we can't recall all of their names. Our turnover rate – around 30% over the past several years – seems far too high. And when you bring in replacements, many of them are gone within 18 months. We've heard you blame our turnover problem on the "lucrative job market," "Gen-Xers," and the "demise of employee loyalty."

To be sure, those factors, which are common in most organizations, have contributed to the situation. And yes, *we* have contributed to the situation, too. But so have you. And we need you to take the lead in reversing this trend.

Keeping good people requires thought and strategies – most of which cost next to nothing.

And we're willing to share a few of our ideas because when good people leave, *we* have to pick up the slack. That means more work for the rest of us ... for the same pay.

Want to know the truth?

One of the main reasons people leave is because management isn't meeting their needs.

Get it? It's not because of pay, benefits, hours, job market, Gen-Xer values, or changing times.

Our pay is competitive. Most benefit packages are generally the same, wherever we look. Work schedules are reasonable. The job market may be good right now, but not so good that we'd leave a job where we're basically happy. And while Gen-Xers may be different in some ways, they tend to have the same basic needs as the rest of the team.

To be candid, many of our peers have left because you, their immediate boss, didn't provide the leadership they needed! Yes, you have more influence over our job satisfaction than anything or anyone else.

> You control the thermostat for the climate in which we work.

Let's get specific. Our workplace climate can be positive and motivating or negative and demotivating, depending on the example you set as a leader. Your leadership style is the single most important variable. It's what separates skyrocketing success from abysmal failure.

This book is written to help you lead us to those successes we all want and need. Please make an effort to really listen to what we have to say and to act on what you hear. If you do, we'll be better employees, who produce better results and deliver better service. Turnover will decrease. You'll be a hero. And together we'll make our organization an extraordinary place to work.

Listen Up, Leader!

We're depending on you to pay attention, improve, and guide!

Contents

How to Get the Most Out of This Book!

U   Read with a highlighter in your hand. Mark key words or phrases that pertain to your personal situation.

U   On page 38, you'll find the CornerStone Principles of Leadership to serve as a guide for your leadership adventure. Refer to them frequently.

U   When you complete this book, order copies for those you lead so they will know that you are listening. This may encourage them to speak up as you listen up.

LISTEN UP!

Character matters!

*A*chieving short-term results doesn't require great leadership. Those kinds of results are easy to get. You can threaten us, pay us more, entice us with contests, manipulate the politics, or trick us in some way. But for us to follow you, long term, our number one requirement is that you be trustworthy. It's even more important than having a great vision, being a great communicator, or being innovative, wise, courageous, inspiring, intelligent, or any other trait you can name.

The first question every person on our team asks is, "Do I trust my boss and the other members of management?" If the answer is "no", then we start looking for someone else to follow – someone we *can* trust. This trust issue is a big deal. It's a by-product of your integrity.

Without integrity, you can never develop trust. Without trust, you will never develop people. Without developing people, you will never maintain a following. And without followers, you have no one to lead. You see, it all begins with integrity.

Okay, so maybe you're thinking: "This is too easy. If I have anything, it's integrity." Most people feel that way. But you may not realize that, far too often, there's a gap between what you think integrity is and what we employees judge your integrity to be.

In our day-to-day experiences, integrity is questioned so frequently that many of us have become callused. In some of our meetings, we've discussed many of the integrity lapses we see in the newspaper almost every day. For 18 months, we talked about the President and wondered how he could lie when he knew the truth would eventually be exposed. In Dallas, the superintendent of schools embezzled $16,000 worth of furniture and lost her $200,000-a-year job. We agreed it was almost unbelievable for her to risk everything she had worked for all of her life, for a mere $16,000!

At one of our meetings, you mentioned that the City of Miami had 33% of its employees on worker's compensation or disability. You laughed when you shared that seven of the workers were out because of paper cuts, of all things.

So we've talked a lot about the integrity of others, but you have never asked us how we judge *your* integrity. That seems strange to us. The most important requirement for any leader is integrity, and we've never had that discussion!

Since we're discussing it now, we'll tell you how we judge your integrity. We don't judge it by major mistakes, like the ones reported in newspapers. But we *do* judge your integrity by what we see – every day.

When you criticize one of our co-workers in public, you lose our trust. When you encourage us to stretch the truth to get an order and say "we'll deal with it later," we question your integrity. When you show favoritism, choose not to return phone calls, say you're out of the office when you are there, or say that you didn't receive a message when you did – all these instances take a toll on our trust in you. As your followers, our integrity questions to you are these:

> "When is a lie small enough that it doesn't matter?"
>
> "Is there a point when 'small' lies are okay but 'big' ones aren't?"
>
> "If so, where is that point ... and how do we know when we cross the line?"

Here's OUR overall answer: No lie is so small that it doesn't matter. The way we see it,

when you sacrifice your integrity, you erode your most precious leadership possession.

Losing your integrity is kind of like boiling a frog.

If you put a frog in boiling water, that frog will immediately realize that it's in danger and will jump out of the pot. But put that same frog in a pot of cold water on the stove and gradually increase the temperature until it boils, and it will remain in the pot, unaware of the subtle temperature changes until it, quite literally, boils to death.

Make sense? Well, that is how you lose your integrity with your team . . . one degree of dishonesty at a time. You see, there are no varying degrees of integrity. We judge whether you have integrity or not based on what we see. You're probably not even aware when you've lost our trust, maybe because you've become immune to the minor lies that have become a major problem for all of us.

As minor as those lies may seem, just remember that we do not forget your integrity mistakes.

We will forget and forgive any judgement error that you make, but integrity mistakes are forever.

So how can you earn our trust and protect your most important leadership tool? Try the following:

1. Keep your promises. You don't have to promise things just to make us feel good. We're more interested in being able to depend on what you promise than in feeling good. Just keep the promises you *do* make and we'll trust what you say.

2. Speak out for what you think is important. We can't read your mind. We don't know how you feel. If we have to guess how you feel about something, we may guess wrong. Please save us the trouble. Tell us how you feel and why. We'll respect you so much more.

3. Err on the side of fairness. Be fair to all of us. We know things are not always clearly right or wrong. Sometimes you have to make difficult decisions that affect many people. Sometimes those decisions include having to de-hire some of us. All we ask is that you be fair at all times – regardless of the type of decisions you have to make.

4. Do what you say you are going to do. Just let your "yes" be yes and your "no" mean no. When you tell us you're going to do something, we should be able to "consider it done."

Are you surprised that we would put integrity this high on our list of priorities?

Most leaders think their followers put vision or communication or problem-solving skills first. Of course, all of those attributes are important, but what difference do they make if we don't trust you? Does it matter what vision you provide if we can't trust that it's best for all of us? Does it matter how well you communicate if we can't trust what you say? Does it matter how charismatic you are if only a handful of us are willing to follow you?

See, it all starts with your integrity. We want you to be successful, just as we want success for ourselves. But we will follow you only if you have earned our trust!

LISTEN UP!

Everything you do counts!

*E*ach of us is an important part of your team.

Why "LISTEN UP" about accountability? Whether you like it or not, the buck stops with you. When a glitch occurs, no one has time for excuses. Taking responsibility is the name of the game – and tag, you're it!

Even though we work for an organization, *you* are our leader. We don't follow the company's mission statement, senior management memos, annual reports, or what the stock market watchers say about us as much as we follow you. And, like it or not, you're not only our leader but also a large part of our career success. Our job happiness depends on our relationship with you.

Please don't take this lightly. Sometimes we lie awake nights worrying about you and how you feel about things. We wonder why you pass us in the hall without even acknowledging our presence. We wonder why you take some of us behind closed doors while leaving others outside. As our leader, you influence all of us!

Believe it or not, we DO understand that leadership isn't easy. We watch every day and see you assume incredible responsibilities. You're accountable for your actions and for *our* actions, plus all the fiscal requirements, employee problems, feedback, training, technology changes, hiring, de-hiring, communicating, staff development, prioritizing, eliminating unnecessary bureaucracy, and much more. Your job is tough. But it is the job you chose.

What we ask of you is to accept responsibility for being the very best at your job so we can be the best at our jobs.

When you became a manager, supervisor, or team leader, the game changed. You're now held to a higher level of accountability than before. In fact, **everything you do is exaggerated; you are under a magnifying glass.** And when you're down, we're down. When you're up, we're up. You set the tone ... you shape the environment in which we can be successful.

Because of this, we expect more from you than from anyone else in our organization. And we need you to lead us without excuses.

The way we see it, when you accepted all the responsibilities of leadership, you lost some of your rights. You lost the right to be cynical or negative, to blame others, to be a member of our "pity parties," and even the right to some of your private time. Everything that happens in our work group is now part of your personal responsibility.

There are a few truths of leadership that you need to know:

First, we are watching everything you do. Even when you think we're not paying attention, we are. There is never a time when you are not leading. You may think that when you choose to ignore an issue, you are not leading. You're wrong! If you show up late for meetings, you lead us to believe that our time isn't valuable. If you lose your cool and over-react to small issues, we wonder how you will react when something big comes along. It's a fact. You are always leading. You can never not lead!

Second, everything you do counts. Sometimes, you may want to share juicy gossip and remove yourself from your leadership role. Don't be fooled. There are no "time outs" with leadership. Everything matters! It's like being on a diet and eating salad all day. Then when you go home, you reward yourself with two pieces of cheesecake because you have been so good. After polishing off the last bite, you try to convince yourself that the cheesecake doesn't matter. Then you weigh yourself ... obviously, it DOES matter! The same is true about your leadership.

And, even though you've been a "professional" all day, don't think that what you say to us away from the office doesn't count. It does!

Third, we have expectations of you. If you're committed to being a great leader, and you want us to be committed followers, there are three things we expect you to do:

- Hire great people. We want teammates who have a desire to be here, a talent for doing the job, and values that fit with our corporate values. Finding and hiring the right people is one of the most important things you do. Take your time. Involve us in the process, and bring in people who will help us be successful. Let's face facts! You can be the greatest manager in the world, but if we have people on our team who are not talented, we will not be successful. We all want to be surrounded with talented people who have skills and abilities to contribute to our success. Don't let us down by hiring any "warm body" just to fill a position. When you do that, it means a lot more work for all of us!

- "De-hire" the people on our team who are not contributing to our mission. We know that letting someone go can't possibly be easy. We're glad *we* don't have that responsibility. But look around. A few of the people on our team are killing us! In fact, they're more detrimental to our success than any of our competitors.

We've seen you ignore the problem, work around the problem, and joke about the problem. You have coached them and done everything you can do. It seems like you spend more time cleaning up after them than recognizing *our* achievements. So get on with it! We're depending on you to provide the best atmosphere for us to be successful. And that includes dealing with problem employees. Be fair, but let them go work somewhere else. If we get lucky, maybe they will find a job with one of our competitors.

Treat us with respect. Our deepest needs are to be understood and to be treated with respect and dignity.

The old Golden Rule should be your number one rule. Just treat us like you would want to be treated if you were in our jobs. Sure, your paycheck may be more than our paychecks. But collectively, you need us just as much as we need you ... sometimes even more.

... it's your responsibility to deal with the problem employees. Be fair, but let them go work somewhere else.

Treat us with dignity and respect. And please ... be sensitive to our needs.

The leadership you display and the decisions that you make contribute more to our success than all other factors combined.

Everything you do counts.
Make it count!

LISTEN UP!

We want to know where we're headed!

*W*ant to know another reason why people leave our company? They're confused about the direction we're going (or not going)!

It may be hard to see from your position, but there's not a lot of clarity – not a lot of direction – in what we're supposed to be doing. Too often, the mission statement hanging on the wall says one thing, you tell us another, and our compensation rewards us for something else.

On top of that, many of our "current" job descriptions were written years ago – in another time, for another purpose. And then when performance reviews come around, you sometimes tell us we should have been doing something completely different. **No wonder we're confused!**

[13]

Believe it or not, many on our team waste as much as five and a half hours a week because of unclear communication about where we're headed and what we're supposed to do. That's seven weeks per year – per person!

If you want to achieve better results and improve our morale, clearly communicate where we are going and why.

There's a secret to retaining employees and achieving results. It's a recipe with four important ingredients:

Ingredient One: Share your vision – what you want us to accomplish. The corporate vision is great for the annual report, but *your* vision is what we need to see. It should be a clear explanation of what our team's results could be and how you see that happening. Help us *want* to follow your lead. Figure out exactly what you want us to accomplish, and we'll help you develop a plan to get it done.

None of us has a crystal ball, and we're not very good at guessing your vision.

So just tell us what it is, and give us a chance to make it happen.

Here's something you may not know: The number one stress we experience comes from not knowing what is expected of us. Despite job descriptions and performance reviews, often we're still unsure of exactly what you expect.

And if you depend on our perceptions to meet your expectations, you're going to be disappointed every time.

When we don't know your expectations, we get side-tracked. We become lost, afraid, and doubting. And internal conflicts develop. Just let us know what you want, and we'll do what you need.

Ingredient Two: Tell us how you think we are doing. Please don't assume that silence on your part tells us we're doing well (as in: if we weren't doing well, you'd let us know). We need to hear from you – whether we're doing things right or wrong! You're not around every time we do a good job, so you can't always tell us. And, as humans, we're all insecure to a certain degree. So we need to hear positive recognition from you. And when you see something you don't like, tell us that, too. We need to know where and how we stand in your eyes.

Ingredient Three: Show us that you care. The question "Does anybody really give a flip around here?" comes up a lot. Recently, a bunch of us talked about what really motivates us to go above and beyond the normal job. **Number one on our list was being appreciated by our boss.** That's right – it came in above money, interesting work, and promotions!

Number two was being involved in the planning stages of things rather than merely implementing decisions other people make.

Number three was working for someone who is empathetic and concerned when we have problems.

Then came money – fourth on the list!

A paycheck doesn't show that leadership cares. Everyone gets a paycheck. What shows us that you care is spending time with us, listening to us, and having a genuine interest in how we are doing – personally as well as professionally.

If you don't *show* us you care, we conclude that you don't. Then we reciprocate ... we stop caring, too.

Ingredient Four: Tell us how our team is doing and where we fit into the bigger picture. We all want to feel like winners. But sometimes we don't know if we're winning or losing because we don't know how the score is being calculated.

Our competitive nature is to win and to contribute to something greater and bigger than just our work group. Give us that opportunity. Show us how you're keeping score and help us learn how to keep score, too. Reward us for winning and help us re-group if we fall down, and we'll be able to reach higher than you ever imagined!

The secret to keeping and motivating us really boils down to communication and building trust. E-mails, voice mails, and memos are all effective methods of communication, but they don't necessarily develop trust. Honestly, we don't think you can develop trust electronically.

Trust happens mostly when there is face-to-face, two-way communication ... and caring.

Okay, so maybe you can get the results you want without a clearly defined vision. It's possible you may get those results whether or not you let us know how we are doing. You can choose NOT to take the time to let us know you care. And you may not think it's important to keep us informed about our team's progress. But this is for sure: There WILL be turnover and poor morale. And you'll be settling for less than our full potential all along the way.

We want to help. Just give us the chance.

LISTEN UP!

What you reward gets done!

Ever wonder why we don't always do what you want? You want us to do a good job, and we *want* to do a good job! It's not rocket science – so why do we sometimes disappoint you with the results we get (or don't get)? Read on!

*O*ne of the primary principles of leadership is that you get what you reward. Sound familiar? Does the name Pavlov ring a bell?

In the past, this principle has worked against our success as much as it has for it. It may sound strange, but sometimes the things that get rewarded around here are not the things you want to happen. In fact, many times the opposite of what you want is the behavior that's rewarded. Doesn't make much sense, does it?

Let me explain – our team is a perfect example:

It's no secret that everyone on our team does not contribute at the same level. Our team performance can be broken down into three groups. About 30% of our team members are top performers – people who will do whatever it takes to get the job done. We also have people who have the talent to do what needs to be done, but choose not to do it all the time. This group represents about 50% of our team. Then there is the other 20% – the unteam players who make no contribution much of the time and actually hinder us from achieving certain goals. Chances are you thought of specific people in each group as you read this paragraph.

So what happens when you have a special project that comes along with a tight deadline? You don't bother with the bottom 20% of our team, do you? No! In fact, you usually don't even involve the middle 50% of our team in the project. It's the top 30% you "reward" with extra work almost every time.

The people you depend on most are the ones you trust, but they are also the ones who get most of the work. We don't blame you for relying on top performers. That's natural. And sometimes the additional work is really okay because high performers tend to want to learn and grow.

But too often, your confidence in the superstars just means more work with no reward. That drives people crazy!

And when it becomes a pattern, top performers begin figuring out how to move into the middle group where they don't have to do the additional work. And the middle group then tries to figure out how to get into the lower group where even less is required. In the end, everyone is working on working LESS. Not good!

If there is no positive "reward" for superb performance, common sense tells you that it will not continue. We've heard several of our peers say that they choose not to do some of your more demanding assignments. When we are actually punished with additional work for doing what you want, we will soon find a way to avoid that punishment. Our sales people say the same thing. They say that the best sales people are "rewarded" with higher and higher sales quotas until they become "average" performers. That just doesn't make any sense to us.

Know what else makes no sense? You failing to deal with the bottom 20% who, too often, get away with murder. When you ignore those who refuse to carry their part of the load, you once again penalize your good performers. Eventually, feeling like we can't win no matter what we do, we stop trying altogether. If and when that happens, you end up losing the most!

Why not just hold each person accountable for his or her performance?

When all is said and done, there are only a few reasons our team may not produce the results you want:

- We're not sure what we should do. If you continually change our mission without telling us, we probably aren't going to meet your expectations. We DO care. But often there is so much ambiguity that we can't figure out where our focus should be. With few exceptions, we will do what you want us to do if we clearly understand what it is and why it is important.

- We don't know how to do it. Yes, training is a big issue around here. Most of us are in our current jobs because we were the best at our previous jobs. But that's no guarantee that we'll be successful at our new positions without training. Teach us how you want things done, give us the tools, and we'll do our best to deliver the results you seek.

- Your reward system is not aligned with our group goals. If we are rewarded for doing a good job and fairly dealt with when we don't, we will do what you want us to do. Just don't punish us for being stars!

- Sometimes YOU present us with obstacles. If we're called into unnecessary meetings, if you interrupt us several times a day, if you ignore our requests for support, we won't be able to get things done as efficiently or effectively as we should.

What you reward, reinforce, and train for is what you will receive. Keep that in mind the next time you strategize on how to get better results.

LISTEN UP!

Don't be afraid to make changes ... be positive!

*C*hange is tough. It's tough for all of us. And we know we don't make it easy for you.

Making necessary changes often means dealing with our complaints and bellyaching. For you, it's probably much easier just to maintain the status quo. But, regardless of how we act, we need changes to help us improve. And we need you to confidently lead us through those changes.

Whoever said "The only constant is change" definitely understood the realities of life ... and of our organization!

A co-worker once said that the only things that don't change are the vending machines in the lunchroom. She was right!

When you bring change to our team, you can pretty much count on resistance. Change is as necessary as breathing, yet most of us would rather take our last breath than move away from our comfort zones. So ...

don't get defensive if we do not immediately accept what you are trying to do. Hang in there with us. The only way we're going to improve is with change. Regardless of how we may resist, we need your leadership ... and your patience.

An old college professor once told us about a study conducted to understand how living beings react to change. Researchers used a mouse and four tubes lying side by side on the floor. They put a cube of cheese in the second tube and released the mouse.

Off he went. When he scurried through the first tube and discovered that it was empty, he quickly went to the second tube. There he found the cheese, ate it, and then went back home. The next day, he did the same thing. Soon he became conditioned: knowing there was no cheese in the first tube, he began going directly to the second tube to get his reward.

After several days, the scientists moved the cheese from the second tube to the third. The mouse was released and, because of his conditioning, went directly to the second tube. But alas, it was empty.

So what do you think he did? Go to the third tube, searching for the cheese? No. Did he go back home? No. Did he decide to go back to the first tube? No. The fourth tube? No again. He stayed in the second tube, waiting for the cheese to appear.

He had become accustomed to finding the cheese in the second tube, and when that changed, he did not adjust. If the scientists had allowed it, the poor mouse probably would have starved.

So what's the point? There are a couple:

First, when things change, we need to make sure we don't "starve to death" waiting for things to go back to the way they were (like the poor mouse). Our comfort zones can be the greatest enemy to our potential. We're depending on you to motivate us away from complacency and keep us from getting so comfortable with the way things are that we cannot adjust to change.

Second, the best time to make change is when things are going well rather than when we're in trouble. If the mouse in the experiment had been searching for more cheese while he was meeting his basic need of survival, he might have discovered a whole block of cheese in the third tube.

Therein lies the paradox of change: The best time to do it is when it seems the least necessary. Why so? Because we're able to deal with it in a positive environment with clear heads, rather than the desperation and sometimes panic of troubled times.

> The Paradox of Change:
> The best time to do it is when it seems the least necessary.

The chances of our team accepting change will improve in proportion to:

- the amount of trust you have earned,
- how much input we have in the change strategy,
- how much we understand about the change, and
- the timing of it all.

Because we're human, it's natural that we'll resist change to some degree. But we need your positive leadership to implement new ideas and to move us all toward improvement.

Speaking of positive leadership, we also need you to maintain a positive attitude – even in times that may be negative and stressful for you. Your attitude has a much greater effect on our team than you probably realize.

When you are positive, we are more positive. When you are negative, we follow your lead.

When you are stressed, we are stressed. We are a reflection of you and your attitude.

People say that there are two enemies of optimism. One is worry, and the other is negative emotion. We depend on you to lead the attack on these enemies and become a positive influence for the rest of us.

Someone in our group noticed that when you are worried about something, our whole team becomes paralyzed because of that worry. We become afraid of the uncertainty we feel and lose our focus on what we are trying to accomplish.

So we're depending on you to stay focused on results; we need you to keep your eye on the goals we are trying to accomplish and look beyond the current and temporary trials we're facing.

It's like when you arrive early at an action movie and walk in to see the last ten minutes of the previous show. You watch the hero and heroine ride off into the sunset, and you know that, regardless of what might have happened before, everything ended happily ever after. Then, when you watch the movie from the beginning, your stress is less, and you can even enjoy the perils facing the heroes.

It's much the same with your leadership. Keep us focused on the results you envision – including changes that need to be made – even when the going gets tough. We need to feel that the tough times we periodically go through are worth the trouble and effort.

If you're like us, chances are that majority of what you worry about never happens. And even if the worst-case scenario occurs, most of what we worry about is out of our control, anyway. So don't fret too much over things beyond your control! When times are difficult, we want to help. If you involve us and share the facts, we will help build a plan of action to make sure the worst doesn't happen.

One last comment about change and being an optimistic leader:

Just like any other work group, our team will have internal conflicts. When those conflicts arise, we're depending on you to address them as soon as you see them happening. If our team is torn apart, nothing good can possibly result. So we ask that you get the facts, offer a reasonable solution, and help us resolve each issue right then.

The longer a problem is allowed to fester within our team, the more energy and emotion it will take to solve.

We all want to see things go smoothly – for you and for us. But even when things are not so positive, we need you to stay focused and to make good things happen.

LISTEN UP!

We want you to take a stand!

*T*ruth be told, we really DO want to be loyal to you and our organization. But you must *earn* our loyalty. We need to be able to count on you to have courage – the courage to take a stand!

While there will always be areas in which we disagree, we should have enough mutual respect that we take the time to understand where we are each coming from – and why.

Your courageous leadership can make a big difference in our success. We need you to have the courage to lead our team to grow, prosper, and become better at what we do!

[29]

Some people say the opposite of courage is cowardliness. Others say it's fear. While both are valid, we think the opposite of courage is conformity. To us, conformity means not having the guts to make decisions that will make us successful.

We're depending on you to exhibit the courage it takes to clear the way for our success. If you want us to follow you – especially in difficult times – you need to:

1. Have the courage to accept responsibility. If you are looking for excuses or someone to blame, we'll never get where we are all trying to go. Blame is looking to the past; responsibility is looking toward the future. We need you to accept responsibility and lead us to that future.

2. Have the courage to seek the truth. Things are not always as they seem. If you don't use all your resources to understand the real truth, you may make bad decisions. The higher you are on the organizational chart, the more difficult it is to discover the truth. We are depending on you to search for the truth and make adjustments based on facts, not perceptions or traditions.

3. Have the courage to take risks. Yes, we want you to take risks – as long as they are well thought out and the end result is worth the price we have to pay. In fact, we'll succeed faster if you will allow us to double our failure rate. Sound strange? You bet it does. But the more we fail, the closer we are to success.

A friend once said, "The definition of profit is reward for risk." We want to profit from our jobs, so we're depending on you to take the risks that are worthwhile ... and allow us to do the same.

4. Have the courage to stand up for what's right. Never forget that we take our cues from you. If you expect us to follow a code of conduct and be intolerant of those who consciously violate that code, then you must do the same. We need you to set the example.

We're willing to take a stand if you are!

5. Have the courage to reject cynics. Hey, there are plenty of cynical people in our world – even in our organization. If you allow them to spread their cynicism, it will eventually take over. We're relying on you to confront the cynics and take action to prevent them from destroying our team.

6. Have the courage to give us freedom to be successful. We want to be the best in our jobs and at what we do. We know it's not always easy to delegate and trust others to do something that you can accomplish yourself, but we need the opportunity to grow. If you don't allow us to experiment and learn, we'll be at the same level two years from now that we are today. We need your courage to allow us to make mistakes and grow from them.

7. Have the courage to persevere. When faced with adversity, often the easiest path is to surrender, to give up. Yet one of the keys to our success is to hang in there longer than everyone else. Don't give up on us or on your vision of success. What separates winners from losers is the courage to persist long enough to win. We're depending on you. Never give up ... or give in!

8. Have the courage to accept the responsibility for your role. You are our leader and role model, everywhere you go and in everything you do. Don't waste your time asking the question "Is anyone watching?" Rather, ask, "What are they seeing and in what direction am I leading?"

   As our leader, you can be an outstanding resource for us. You can communicate with all levels of the organization. You can help us find solutions to our problems. You can create an atmosphere in which we can all succeed in our work.

Never doubt that your leadership is needed. We depend on you to maintain a sharp customer focus by building relationships with internal and external customers – utilizing every resource to improve their levels of satisfaction. We rely on you to help us achieve business objectives and to succeed – no matter how great the challenge. We expect you to live by a code of conduct and to retain your personal and business integrity. It requires courage to take a stand and accept responsibility as our leader. Just remember that the result of your courage is the influence that you have on us. Please don't take that lightly.

LISTEN UP!

We want to work for the best!

*T*he fact is, we didn't choose you to be our boss. And you didn't hire most of us who are working for you now. But, regardless of how we all ended up on the same team, we DO have expectations of each other.

One of the expectations we have of you is to be the very best. We want you to grow and achieve so that we'll have that same opportunity. Having worked for many different people in the past, we believe we have a pretty good read on what separates the best leaders from the mediocre ones. One important factor is a commitment to learning and improving.

We're depending on you to know more than our competitors, and to push *us* to know more than they do, too.

Take time to learn! Just because you're a manager doesn't mean that your learning has peaked or ended. In fact, you are now challenged to learn more rapidly so that you can share that learning with others.

If you create an environment for learning, we will develop and become more skillful.

Establish a book library, and we will read. Offer us audio tapes, and we will listen. Send us to seminars, and we will bring back good ideas to share with our team.

Teach us how to lead so that we will become more committed and begin preparing ourselves for the next step in our careers. Reward learning, and we will be hungry to learn more.

Finally, as our leader, we want you to enjoy your job and have balance in your life. You spend far too much time with us not to take pleasure in what you're doing. When you are happy, we are happy. When you are stressed, we are stressed. As we said before, you set the tone for the entire workplace. Don't take that responsibility lightly, but don't take yourself too seriously, either.

If you achieve all of your work goals but lose your family in the process, you won't be the kind of person we want to follow. If you abuse substances to help you cope with our challenges, our respect will quickly be replaced with pity or disdain. If you move up the ladder quickly but trade off your health to do so, you won't be the role model we need.

We want you to succeed as much as you want the same for us – but not at any price. You need to be successful in ALL areas of your life: personal, physical, spiritual, emotional, and professional. Without this important balance, you cannot lead us. You see, we will follow only the best.

You have chosen to play a special role in our lives. We need you ... we depend on you.

Our purpose in writing this book has been to contribute ideas that will improve morale, retention, loyalty, and customer satisfaction.

Our sincere hope is that you will LISTEN UP so we can all achieve extraordinary results!

A closing thought ...

*L*eadership can't be claimed like luggage at the airport. Leadership can't be inherited, even though you may inherit a leadership position. There are no manufacturing plants that fabricate leadership. And leadership can't be given as a gift – even if you've been blessed with an abundance of leadership skills to share with someone else. Leadership must be EARNED by mastering a defined set of skills and by working with others to achieve common goals.

May your journey as a leader bring success, balance to your life, and an increasingly clear vision of the opportunities presented in the New Millennium.

David Cottrell

The CornerStone
Principles of Leadership

VALUES PRINCIPLES

The Principle of Integrity – Results improve in proportion to the level of trust earned by the leader.

The Principle of Responsibility – Results improve when leaders and their followers are held accountable for their actions.

The Principle of Commitment – Results improve to the extent that the leader hires and develops talented people.

The Principle of Vision – Results improve when leaders establish a crystal-clear vision with a convincing reason to embrace the vision.

SYNERGY PRINCIPLES

The Principle of Communication – Results improve when followers understand their role and are rewarded for their accomplishments.

The Principle of Conflict Resolution – Results improve when the leader timely removes obstacles inhibiting followers.

The Principle of Optimism – Results improve in proportion to the self-esteem and attitude of the leader.

The Principle of Change Management – Results improve to the extent that the leader embraces change and makes change positive.

INVESTMENT PRINCIPLES

The Principle of Empowerment – Results improve as followers are allowed to accept responsibility for their actions.

The Principle of Courage – Results improve in proportion to the leader's ability to confront issues affecting their followers.

The Principle of Example – Results improve when the leader is a positive role model.

The Principle of Preparation – Results improve to the extent that leaders develop themselves and their followers.

Special thanks ...

... to the following friends and customers who have provided the opportunity to LISTEN UP and learn from their ideas and wisdom:

Alice Adams	Kevin Marshall
Ken Byrd	Bill McHale
Ken Carnes	Joe Miles
Phil Childress	Jeanne O'Neill
Dr. David Cook	Fred Roach
Keith Crabtree	Mark Shackelford
Paul Damoc	Tod Taylor
Bryan Dodge	Bryan Tracy
Ed Foreman	Tony Van Roekel
Eric Harvey	Steve Ventura
Johnny Koons	DeFae Weaver
Louis Krueger	John Winkelman

And a very special thanks to

Mark Layton

for his creativity, encouragement,
and incredible vision.

The WALK THE TALK® Company

Since 1977, The WALK THE TALK Company has helped organizations achieve success through Ethical Leadership and Values-Based Business practices. And we're ready to do the same for you!

Through keynote and conference presentations, customized training and consulting, and high-imapct publications like David Cottrell's

Listen Up, Leader!

we have become one of the world's most respected providers of Ethics and Values-Based Business Resources.

The Author

David Cottrell, President and CEO of CornerStone Leadership, is an internationally known leadership consultant and speaker. His business experience includes senior management positions with Xerox and FedEx. He also led the successful turnaround of a chapter eleven company before founding CornerStone.

Like to bring David Cottrell and his powerful Listen UP, Leader! message to your next conference or leadership development event? Call us today at 1.888.822.9255 or e-mail us at info@walkthetalk.com to learn more!

Other WALK THE TALK Resources

Ethics4Everyone is a unique and powerful resource for employees at ALL levels. It provides practical information to guide individual actions, decisions, and daily behaviors. — $9.95

Nuts'nBolts LEADERSHIP provides practical, easy-to-follow "how-to's" to help your people meet their most challenging leadership responsibilities. — $9.95

144 Ways to Walk the Talk – Quick-reference handbook packed with 144 techniques and strategies to help you build a high performance organization. — $9.95

Walking The Talk Together – Focusing on shared responsibility, this easy-read handbook encourages employees to be accountable for values-driven business practices. — $9.95

180 Ways to Walk the Leadership Talk – Quick reference handbook designed to help current and future leaders build a values-centered organization. — $9.95

The Manager's Coaching Handbook is a practical guide to improve the performance of your "super stars, middle stars, and falling stars". — $9.95

Walk Awhile In MY Shoes – Revolutionary handbook that helps you break down we vs. they beliefs that exist between "bosses and workers". — $9.95

Monday Morning Leadership offers unique encouragement and direction that will help you become a better manager, employee, and person. — $12.95

180 Ways To Walk The Recognition Talk – Proven techinques and practical strategies will get everyone "walking the recognition talk!!!" — $9.95

WALK THE TALK ... And Get The Results You Want (recently released softcover) – Bring new energy to your organization! This book will help you build a culture of ethics and values-based business practices. — $12.95

Please send me extra copies of: Listen UP, Leader!

1-99 copies $9.95 each   100-499 copies $9.45 each   500+ copies please call

| Listen UP, Leader! | ____ copies X | ____ | =$_____ |

Additional Leadership Development Books

Ethics4Everyone	____ copies X	$ 9.95	=$_____
Nuts'nBolts LEADERSHIP	____ copies X	$ 9.95	=$_____
144 Ways To Walk The Talk	____ copies X	$ 9.95	=$_____
Walking The Talk Together	____ copies X	$ 9.95	=$_____
180 Ways To Walk The Leadership Talk	____ copies X	$ 9.95	=$_____
The Manager's Coaching Handbook	____ copies X	$ 9.95	=$_____
Walk Awhile In *MY* Shoes	____ copies X	$ 9.95	=$_____
Monday Morning Leadership	____ copies X	$ 12.95	=$_____
180 Ways To Walk The Recognition Talk	____ copies X	$ 9.95	=$_____
WALK THE TALK ... And Get The Results You Want *(available April 2003)*	____ copies X	$ 12.95	=$_____
	Product Total		$_____
	*Shipping & Handling		$_____
	Subtotal		$_____
	Sales Tax:		$_____
(Sales & Use Tax Collected on TX & CA Customers Only)	Texas Sales Tax – 8.25%		$_____
	CA Sales & Use Tax		$_____
	Total (U.S. Dollars Only)		**$_____**

*Shipping and Handling Charges

6% plus $4.00 of the "Product Total." Orders are shipped ground delivery 7-10 days. Next and 2nd business day delivery available – call 888.822.9255. Call 972.243.8863 for quote if outside continental U.S.

Name_____ Title_____

Organization_____

Shipping Address_____

City_____ State_____ Zip _____

Phone_____ Fax_____

E-Mail_____

Charge Your Order: ❑ MasterCard   ❑ Visa   ❑ American Express

Credit Card Number_____Exp. Date_____

❑ Check Enclosed (Payable to The WALK THE TALK Company)

❑ Please Invoice **(Orders over $250 ONLY)**   ❑ P.O. Number (if applicable)_____

PHONE	FAX
1.888.822.9255	972-243-0815
or 972.243.8863	ON-LINE
M-F, 8:30-5:00 Cen.	www.walkthetalk.com

MAIL
WALK THE TALK Co.
2925 LBJ Fwy., #201
Dallas, TX 75234

Please let us know if you would like to learn more about ...

❑ Keynote Presentations and Leadership Development Training by David Cottrell

❑ *Ethics4Everyone* "Training In A Box"

❑ The WALK THE TALK Success Series Training Package

❑ Other WALK THE TALK Handbooks

❑ The WALK THE TALK On-line 360° Feedback Process

❑ 360° Feedback customized for your organization's mission, vision, and values

Please supply us with your email address:

Helping organizations achieve success through Ethical Leadership and Values-Based Business Practices

The WALK THE TALK® Company
2925 LBJ Freeway • Suite 201 • Dallas, Texas 75234
972.243.8863 • Fax 972.243.0815 • **www.walkthetalk.com**